LUNG

LUNG and T ⟶ ꞏꞏꞏⁿⁿ

WOODHILL

by Matt Woodhead

WOODHILL

by Matt Woodhead

CAST

Lee	Tyler Brazao
Janet	Marina Climent
Ghost	Chris Otim
Carole	Miah Robinson

AUDIO CAST

Lee	Delroy Atkinson
Carole	Clare Corbett
Janet	Julie Jupp
Ghost	Corey Montague-Sholay

ENSEMBLE AUDIO CAST

Joey Akubeze
Komal Amin
Philip Arditti
Crystal Condie
Jonathan Coote
Kay Eluvian
Souad Faress
Luke Francis
Sanchia McCormack
Helen Monks
Raad Rawi
Sid Sagar
Laura Dos Santos
Bianca Stephens
Liyah Summers
Jessica Temple
Maanuv Thiara
Thomas Wheatley

CREATIVE TEAM

Assistant Director	Madiha Ansari
Associate Director	Gitika Buttoo
Sound Designer	Owen Crouch
Composer and Sound Engineer	Sami El-Enany
Wellbeing Coordinator and Counsellor	Ruth Hannant
Producer	Camille Koosyial
Dramaturg	Helen Monks
Lighting Designer	Will Monks
Poster Designer	Alex Powell
Costume Supervisor	Megan Rarity
Choreographer	Alexzandra Sarmiento
Set and Costume Designer	Lulu Tam
Writer and Director	Matt Woodhead

PRODUCTION TEAM

Production Manager	Lisa Hood
Technical Stage Manager	Jay Hirst
Company Stage Manager	Thomas Manly

ACADEMIC ADVISORS

Dr Gill Buck
Professor Philippa Tomczak

WOODHILL FAMILIES GROUP

Carole Carpenter
Janet Farrar
Sophia Farrar
Lee Jarman
Linda Stokes

ACKNOWLEDGEMENTS

Interviewees

A big thank you to everyone who shared their story. It takes courage and strength to speak about something as tender as death in prison. This play would not have been possible without you.

Supporters

Thank you to all of the supporters of this project: Joyce Adeyanju, Katie Battcock, Shahida Begum, Deborah Best, Alecky Blythe, Jack Butterworth, Susannah Bramwell, Hannah Bristow, Ellie Browning, Beth Byrne, Ruby Chandler, Sarah Clarke, Ellie Claughton, Jo Eggleton, David Edgar, Christine Edzard, Andrew Faux, Tom Forster, Richard Goodwin, David Graham, Ruby Greenwood, Simon Hattenstone, Colin Henderson, John Hoggarth, Clive Holland, John Holmwood, Ethan Hudson, Suzy Humphries, Brian Hutchinson, Abbie Howell, Hannah Jackson, Karim Khan, Nadia Lakhani, Yami Löfvenberg, Lizzie Mounter, Richard Norton-Taylor, Oluwatosin Omotosho, Kirsty Patrick-Ward, Alex Powell, Olivier Stockman, Joe Thornber, Chris Thorpe, Ephraim Tshibemba, Zoe Vail, Gemma Wilson, Susan Wright.

Thank you to everyone at Faber, Front Seat Media, Inquest, Sands Films Studio, Summerhall, Shoreditch Town Hall, The Sit Up Awards and Mobius for supporting the development of this play.

Our Funders

We are grateful for the support of the following trusts, foundations and organisations: Arts Council England, Austin and Hope Pilkington Trust, Blakemore Foundation, Lush Community Fund, National Lottery Community Fund, Raymond Williams Foundation, Royal Victoria Hall, University of Nottingham, The Reflective Practice, WO Street Charitable Foundation and the Writers' Guild.

Additional Credits

The commissioning of *Woodhill* was enabled by a grant from the New Play Commission Scheme, a project set up by the Writers' Guild of Great Britain, UK Theatre and the Independent Theatre Council, and funded by Arts Council England, the Theatre Development Trust and donations from actors, directors, playwrights and producers.

Woodhill was developed with the support of the National Theatre.

BIOGRAPHIES

CAST

Tyler Brazao – Lee

Tyler trained at The BRIT School and Bird College. He has danced on *Britain's Got Talent* and *The X Factor*. Selected credits include: *Sleeping Beauty* (Hazlitt Theatre); *Beauty and the Beast* (Imagine Theatre); *Beats 372* (Creative Blood).

Marina Climent – Janet

Marina is a professional dancer from Barcelona. She trained in jazz, ballet, contemporary and commercial. Selected credits include: *Wonderland in Alice* (CTC Dance Company); *Pumpkin Lab* (Bluestone); *Tara vs Bilal* (JA Entertainment); *Identity* (Theatre Peckham, CTC Dance Company).

Chris Otim – Ghost

Chris trained at Urdang Academy. Selected credits include: *Aida* (Royal Opera House); *Snow White and the Seven Dwarfs* Pantomimes); *Lean On* (Shan Ako/Claudimar Neto). Workshops include: *Cinderella* (Matthew Bourne, New Adventures); *Charge* (Motionhouse); *Groove on Down the Road* (ZooNation).

Miah Robinson – Carole

Miah is a movement artist in West London. Her aspiration is to be knowledgeable, versed in all styles and their foundations, aiming to not be confined by the aforementioned. She wants her contribution to the industry to be uplifting, building and encouraging. *Woodhill* is Miah's professional debut.

CREATIVE TEAM

Madiha Ansari – Assistant Director

Madiha is an actor and facilitator from West Yorkshire. Selected credits include: *Vitamin D* (Saher Shah, UK tour); *Full English* (Bent Architect); *PicknMix* (Leeds Studio, Pleasance); *Trojan Horse* (LUNG, UK tour); *Dreamliners* (The Situationalists, Edinburgh).

Awards include: Diversity Champion (Kirklees); UK Creative Award (British Council); Best Animation (RTS, Fettle).

Gitika Buttoo – Associate Director

Gitika is a queer British South Asian director from Yorkshire, currently based in Manchester. Selected credits include: *Road* (Oldham Coliseum); *Love N Stuff* (Watford Palace and Sheffield Theatres); *A Force to Be Reckoned With* (Mikron Theatre, UK tour); *The Jungle Book* (Storyhouse Theatre); *The Father and the Assassin* (National Theatre) as Staff Director. Awards include: Best Online Audio Production (Off West End Awards); Best Stage Production (nominee, Asian Media Awards).

Owen Crouch – Sound Designer

Owen studied Sound Arts and Design at London College of Communication (University of the Arts London). Selected credits include: *After the Act* (New Diorama); *Trojan Horse* (Summerhall, UK tour); *Gulliver's Travels* (Unicorn Theatre); *The Witchfinder's Sister* (Queen's Theatre Hornchurch); *BU21* (Trafalgar Studios). Awards include: Off West End Award Finalist for Sound and Music on *Gulliver's Travels*; Amnesty International Freedom of Expression Award; Fringe First for *Trojan Horse*.

Sami El-Enany – Composer and Sound Engineer

Sami El-Enany is an artist who works with sound, often negotiating the fringes of modern classical, electronica and found sound. His work has filled spaces including the Barbican, ICA, National Theatre, Tate and South London Gallery. Selected credits include: *Creation of the Birds* (radio drama, 2022, Falling Tree Productions); *Deadly Structures* (videogame, 2022, ICA + BBC); *Walking with Shadows* (narrative feature film, OYA Media); *The Book of Harth* (documentary feature, 2022, Shadow Court Productions); *Opix* (LP, 2020, Faith and Industry Imprint). Selected awards include: Grand Prix Nova, 2023; Best Radio Drama for *Creation of the Birds*; Best Score at Independent International Film Festival, for *Latent*.

Ruth Hannant – Wellbeing Coordinator and Counsellor

Ruth is a BACP Registered Counsellor who trained at Leeds Becket University (PG Dip) and graduated with a BA (Hons) in Arts Management from DeMontfort University, Leicester. Ruth runs a private practice in therapeutic counselling. Prior to this, she worked in theatre for nearly 25 years specialising in finding pathways for non-traditional audiences to feel at home in their local theatre. Ruth's most recent theatre role was as Head of Creative Engagement at Leeds Playhouse where she was instrumental in creating the first Theatre of Sanctuary, supporting refugees and people seeking asylum. Ruth is also a director of a local music school, LS18 Rocks, for children and adults.

Camille Koosyial – Producer

Camille is a British Guyanese Creative Producer from South West London. She is currently the Producer for LUNG and studied at Chris O'Grady Institute of Creative Producing and the University of East Anglia. Selected credits include: *My Uncle is Not Pablo Escobar* (Brixton House); *Hot in Here* (Gate Theatre and UK tour); *The Children's Inquiry* (National Theatre Studio); *The Family Sex Show* (The Egg).

Helen Monks – Dramaturg

Helen is a writer, actor and the Co-Artistic Director of LUNG. She co-wrote *E15*, which has been on two UK tours and was published by Bloomsbury. Her play *Trojan Horse* (co-written with Matt Woodhead) was developed with Leeds Playhouse. Selected acting credits include: *Upstart Crow*, *Inside No. 9* (BBC 2); *Election Spy* (BBC 1); *Genius* (21st Century Fox); *Raised By Wolves* (Channel 4). Selected awards include: Amnesty International Freedom of Expression Award; Fringe First; Sit-Up Award for Social Engagement.

Will Monks – Lighting Designer

Will trained at the Bristol Old Vic Theatre School. Selected credits include: *Foxes* (59E59 in New York, Theatre 503, Seven Dials Playhouse); *Out of Her Mouth* (UK tour); *The MP, Aunty Mandy & Me* (UK tours); *Far Gone* (international tour); *Petula* (National Theatre Wales).

Megan Rarity – Costume Supervisor

Megan trained at Arts University Bournemouth in Costume for Performance Design. Selected credits include: *Indecent Proposal the Musical* (Southwark Playhouse); *Camp Siegfried* (The Old Vic); *The Two-Character Play* (Hampstead Theatre); *Last Easter* (Orange Tree Theatre); *Shedding a Skin* (Soho Theatre).

Alexzandra Sarmiento – Choreographer

Alexzandra trained at the LaGuardia High School of Art & Performing Arts in New York City. Selected choreography credits includes: *How to Succeed in Business Without Really Trying* (Southwark Playhouse); *Brief Encounter* (New Wolsey Theatre and UK tour); *Addams Family* (Mountview); *42 Balloons* (Vaudeville); *But I'm a Cheerleader* (Turbine). As a performer, selected theatre credits include: *Message in a Bottle* (ZooNation, International tour); original London company of *Hamilton* (Victoria Palace); *Jekyll & Hyde* (The McOnie Company, The Old Vic).

Lulu Tam – Set and Costume Designer

Lulu trained at the Royal Central of Speech and Drama, and she is a teaching fellow at the University of Salford. Selected credits include: *The Killing of Sister George* (Told by An Idiot and New Vic Theatre); *A Pretty Shitty Love* (Theatr Clwyd); *The Prince* (Southwark Playhouse); *This is Paradise* (Traverse Theatre); *Lit* (Nottingham Playhouse, High Tide Festival); *A Winter's Tale* (Les Kurbas Theatre). Awards include: Linbury Prize (finalist); World Stage Design 2017; Naomi Wilkinson Award for Stage Design 2022 (winner).

Matt Woodhead – Director and Writer

Matt trained on the National Theatre Studio Directors Course and as a Trainee Director at Leeds Playhouse. Selected credits include: *The 56* (UK tour); *E15* (Battersea Arts Centre and UK tour); *Chilcot* (The Lowry); *Who Cares* (The Lowry and UK tour); *Trojan Horse* (Leeds Playhouse and UK tour). Selected awards include: Director's Guild Award for Best Newcomer, John Fernald Award, Fringe First, Amnesty International Freedom of Expression Award.

PRODUCTION TEAM

Lisa Hood – Production Manager

Lisa trained in Theatre Arts at Middlesex University. Selected credits include: *The Flying Dutchman* (Opera Up Close UK tour); *My Uncle is Not Pablo Escobar* (Brixton House); *An Octoroon* (Orange Tree Theatre); *Jess and Joe Forever* (UK tour).

Jay Hirst – Technical Stage Manager

Jay began their career at Hull Truck Theatre and has since toured extensively across the UK, working with companies such as Stephen Joseph Theatre and Northern Broadsides. Selected credits include: *Modest* (Middle Child/Milk Presents); *Sherlock Holmes: The Valley of Fear* (Blackeyed Theatre, UK tour); *The Fellowship* (Hampstead Theatre); *Everything I See I Swallow* (Shasha & Taylor Productions, UK tour); *One Day, Maybe* (dreamthinkspeak).

Thomas Manly – Company Stage Manager

Tom trained as an actor at St Mary's University, before pursuing a career in Stage Management. Selected credits include: *Jekyll and Hyde* (National Theatre tour); *Shut up, I'm Dreaming* (National Theatre in collaboration with The PappyShow).

ACADEMIC ADVISORS

Dr Gill Buck – Academic Advisor

Dr Gill Buck is an Associate Professor at the University of Chester. She is a qualified social worker with over ten years' experience in social work and related practices. Gill spent most of her career as a social worker in the Youth Offending Service. Prior to this, she worked supporting young people who were sexually exploited; as a support worker with recently arrived asylum seekers; and as a volunteer counsellor for Rape Crisis. Gill's teaching interests include user informed services, criminal justice, critical approaches to practise, theories of human interaction and research methods.

Professor Philippa Tomczak – Academic Advisor

Philippa is a Principal Research Fellow at the University of Nottingham and holds a UKRI Future Leaders Fellowship and ERC Starting Grant. She directs the Prisons, Health and Societies Research Group and has been undertaking research and impact work with the Prisons and Probation Ombudsman since 2019. Her expertise is in punishment, specifically: prison suicide, investigating deaths in criminal justice detention, regulating criminal justice detention, the penal voluntary sector, charitable involvement in (criminal) justice, actor-network theory and document analysis.

WOODHILL FAMILIES GROUP

Carole, Janet, Lee, Linda and Sophia are five people whose loved ones died at HMP Woodhill. They have all met once a month for the last year to form the Woodhill Families Group. Carole is a Learning Support Assistant and her happy place is chilling in bed with the telly on. Janet is the loving mother of four incredible children who she will travel to the ends of the earth to see. Sophia is training to be an electrician and she has just become the proud owner of four adorable baby kittens. Lee is a drum and bass enthusiast and a wicked blacksmith. Linda was born in Bombay, she loves going out for a drink with the girls and she has a heart of absolute gold.

LUNG

Founded in Barnsley in 2012, LUNG are a verbatim theatre company that tours work nationally. LUNG creates work that shines a light on political, social and economic issues in modern Britain using people's actual words to tell their stories. LUNG are Partners at The Lowry and Creative Associates with National Theatre Learning.

'Infectious'
★ ★ ★ ★
London Evening Standard on *E15*

'Superb'
★ ★ ★ ★
The Scotsman on *Who Cares*

'Piercing, relevant, terrifying and beautifully told'
★ ★ ★ ★ ★
WhatsOnStage on *Trojan Horse*

LUNG are winners of the Amnesty International Freedom of Expression Award, Sit-Up Award for social impact and Fringe First Award.

CORE TEAM

Madia Ansari	LUNG Creative
Gitika Buttoo	Associate Director
Maggie Fowler	Fundraiser
Camille Koosyial	Producer
Helen Monks	Co-Director
Matt Woodhead	Co-Director

BOARD

Shazad Amin	Trustee
Inga Hirst	Trustee
Zeena Rasheed	Chair of the board
Deborah Rees	Trustee
Gilly Roche	Trustee
Rhiannon McKay Smith	Trustee

To find out more, visit www.lungtheatre.co.uk or follow us at @lungtheatre.

The North Wall
Arts Centre

The award-winning North Wall Arts Centre opened in 2007, and brings together artists and audiences from Oxford and beyond to make, share and experience art of the highest quality. Comprising a theatre, gallery and studio spaces, the venue's public programme places an emphasis on contemporary work, amplifying diverse voices and providing a platform for untold stories.

Alongside its programming, The North Wall supports artists through its ArtsLab programme, which offers established and early-career artists the chance to develop and showcase new work through residencies, mentorship and training.

In addition to this, the venue runs a participation programme with children, young people and families at its heart; forging long-term partnerships with local schools and community groups to co-create projects which bring people together through creative opportunities.

The North Wall is grateful for the continued support of its principal sponsor, St Edward's School.

CORE TEAM

Director	Ria Parry
Deputy Director	Amy Walters
Technical Manager	Clive Stevenson
Participation Manager	Abigail Walton
Gallery Manager	Nicky Laird
General Manager	Wendy Weiss
Associate Producer	Amelia Thornber
Senior Technician	James Bailey
Front of House Manager	Gabi Wilson
Front of House Supervisors	Tenika Blake, Ethan Powell and Stella Harford

The North Wall Trust is a limited company and registered charity.
Registered company no: 07951538, Registered charity no: 1146851

The North Wall Arts Centre, South Parade, Oxford OX2 7JN
Tel: 01865 319 450
thenorthwall.com
@thenorthwall

Woodhill

Matt Woodhead trained on the National Theatre Studio
Directors Course and as a Trainee Director at Leeds
Playhouse. Selected credits include: *The 56* (UK tour), *E15*
(Battersea Arts Centre and UK tour), *Chilcot* (The Lowry),
Who Cares (The Lowry and UK tour), *Trojan Horse* (Leeds
Playhouse and UK tour). Selected awards include: Director's
Guild Award for Best Newcomer, John Fernald Award,
Fringe First, Amnesty International Freedom of Expression
Award.

MATT WOODHEAD

Woodhill

faber

First published in 2023
by Faber and Faber Limited
The Bindery, 51 Hatton Garden
London, ECIN 8HN

Typeset by Brighton Gray
Printed and bound in the UK by CPI Group (Ltd), Croydon CR0 4YY

A CIP record for this book
is available from the British Library

ISBN 978-0-571-38851-6

MIX
Paper | Supporting
responsible forestry
FSC® C013604
www.fsc.org

Printed and bound in the UK on FSC® certified paper in line with our continuing
commitment to ethical business practices, sustainability and the environment.
For further information see faber.co.uk/environmental-policy

2 4 6 8 10 9 7 5 3

Contents

Foreword

For over four decades INQUEST, an independent charity, has supported countless families whose loved ones have died in prisons, working alongside them through the distressing and protracted processes that follow. INQUEST shines a light on the systemic issues involved in the deaths of people in the care of the state, and tells the human stories of those who have died. *Woodhill* tells these stories in an innovative and captivating way.

In the last thirty years, the prison population has ballooned by 75 per cent, with Britain having the highest imprisonment rate in Western Europe. The de-facto policy of prison expansion across successive governments has been accompanied by a rising tide of morally indefensible deaths in prison. People in prison are some of the most marginalised in society, with experiences of institutional care, homelessness, educational disadvantage, addiction, mental and physical ill health, and abuse, underpinned by poverty and inequality. Many have been failed by other statutory agencies long before entering the criminal justice system. This is most strongly felt across the intersections of race, gender, class, sexuality and disability.

The deplorable situation at Woodhill Prison, where twenty-nine people have taken their own lives since 2011, is a stark example of a much wider national issue. What was uncovered at Woodhill, and is seen in prisons across the country, are shocking levels of systemic failure, neglect and despair.

The families of those who die engage in post-death processes and campaigning, with the aim of ending preventable and premature deaths. A constant stream of prison inspectorate reports, inquiries, and inquest findings have produced rigorous recommendations to better protect the health and safety of prisoners. Yet these are systematically ignored, resulting in more deaths in disturbingly similar circumstances. This led INQUEST to launch an ongoing campaign called No More Deaths. We are calling for a National Oversight Mechanism: an independent body tasked with following up on recommendations arising from deaths. The Mechanism would ensure greater transparency and accountability, with the potential to save lives.

As an adviser to Clean Break theatre company, working with women who have experience of the criminal justice system, I have seen how theatre is a powerful tool of resistance, which can radically challenge injustice and inequality. *Woodhill* by LUNG deftly weaves together the stories of imprisoned people, the experiences of bereaved families and the broader socio-political context to create a richly textured fabric of life and death in prison. It engages with the grief and anger of those affected that the legal process tends to steamroll.

We hope that that this production mobilises people to question the appropriateness of prison as a response to social issues and to consider how redirecting resources away from the criminal justice system, towards communities and to welfare, health, housing, education and social care, can better address the root causes of harm and violence. *Woodhill* represents an opportunity to bear witness to the pain and struggle of bereaved families and people in prison, and to support them and INQUEST in our continued fight for truth, justice and accountability and meaningful societal change.

Deborah Coles
Director of INQUEST

Author's Note

Grief haunts our lives in different ways. An empty seat at the dinner table, a crossed-out birthday reminder in your calendar, an intrusive thought when the lights are out and you're trying to sleep. I don't think we ever truly lose someone when they die. Memories and fragments of them creep into our lives every day.

Writing this play has been a privilege and life-changing experience. For the last few years, I've worked with three families whose loved ones died at HMP Woodhill. Carole, Janet, Lee, Linda and Sophia have come together from different paths of life to form a group. We've laughed, cried and spoken about three special people who are no longer with us. Three young men who were sent to prison and never came home: Chris, Stephen and Kevin.

In our monthly sessions, we speak about these men in the present tense. I never met Chris, Stephen or Kevin, but here are some of the things I've heard about them over early morning coffees and late-night phone calls. I will speak about these men as they *are,* not who they *were.*

Chris is a cheeky chappy and a little bit vain. A good-looking lad, he loves checking himself out in the mirror and telling everyone, 'I've still got it.' Stephen is a rugby player and father to two beautiful children. I've heard so many stories about how proud he is of the people they have become. Kevin is the worst career criminal going. His first offence was stealing his girlfriend's dildo. Who knew that she would call the police?

These three men live on because their families are determined to make it so. Chris's ashes are engraved in the jewellery his family wears. A part of him sits on his mother's wrist and hangs around his sister's neck. Stephen lives on in tattoos. Inked onto his sister's neck and his mother's foot, he walks with his loved ones every day. Kevin lives on in his stepbrother's heart, which beats relentlessly for justice.

What is tragic about the deaths of these three men is that it was all avoidable. There are three empty seats at the dinner table. Decades of birthdays crossed out of the calendar. Thousands of sleepless nights. Chris, Stephen and Kevin shouldn't be living in jewellery and tattoos. These men should be living among us and breathing the air we breathe. The only reason they aren't is because the state made it so.

Carole, Janet, Lee, Linda and Sophia have bared their souls to make this play. Standing shoulder to shoulder with them has made me see the grief that has unknowingly eclipsed my own life. It's also made me see that grief is a powerful thing. When shared and channelled, it can be a radical thing.

Read these families' stories. Hear their words. Watch as they turn their grief into an act of resistance.

Matt Woodhead

'Our boys needed help, not punishment. They were given a
prison sentence that turned into a death sentence.
There is a crisis unfolding in our prisons.
We will not stop until their story is heard.'

Carole, Janet, Lee, Linda and Sophia

Woodhill was produced by LUNG and The North Wall Arts Centre, Oxford, and first performed at The North Wall on 27 July 2023. The cast was as follows:

Lee Tyler Brazao
Janet Marina Climent
Ghost Chris Otim
Carole Miah Robinson

Audio performers
Lee Delroy Atkinson
Carole Clare Corbett
Janet Julie Jupp
Ghost Corey Montague-Sholay

Ensemble audio performers
Joey Akubeze, Komal Amin, Philip Arditti, Crystal Condie, Jonathan Coote, Kay Eluvian, Souad Faress, Luke Francis, Sanchia McCormack, Helen Monks, Raad Rawi, Sid Sagar, Laura Dos Santos, Bianca Stephens, Liyah Summers, Jessica Temple, Maanuv Thiara, Thomas Wheatley

Assistant Director Madiha Ansari
Associate Director Gitika Buttoo
Sound Designer Owen Crouch
Composer and Sound Engineer Sami El-Enany
Wellbeing Coordinator and Counsellor Ruth Hannant
Producer Camille Koosyial
Dramaturg Helen Monks
Lighting Designer Will Monks
Costume Supervisor Megan Rarity
Choreographer Alexzandra Sarmiento
Set and Costume Designer Lulu Tam
Writer and Director Matt Woodhead

Characters

Janet

Lee

Carole

Ghost

Ensemble

Resident, Prison Officer, Zoom, Prison Service, A3745JF,
A2001RN, Nurse 1, Nurse 2, Nurse 3, Victim Support
Worker, Magistrate, Volunteer, Chaplain, Chris's Mum,
Academic, Architect, Lord, Minister, Inspector, Family
Liaison Officer, Visitor, Dealer, Governor, National
Chairman, Investigator, Education Tutor, Daughter,
Grendon, Wandsworth, Brixton, Chief Inspectorate,
Ombudsman, Dad, Police Officer, Council Worker, Fellow,
Mum, Advocate, Charity Director, Campaigner, Myatt,
Solicitor, Legal Adviser, Barrister, Partner

Setting

*A warehouse which stores and imposes memories of grief.
In the play, three worlds intertwine. The living world (vivid
memories of the past), limbo (a liminal space where the
characters are suspended in time) and the otherworld
(where external voices intrude on the action on stage).*

WOODHILL

Notes

Adapted from interviews, this play is written for dance. All the text has been pre-recorded by actors and set to music. The final scene is performed by the real voices of Janet, Lee and Carole.

Through the play, the dancers do not speak on stage. Ignored and unheard, bereaved families who have lost a family member in prison often feel like no one is listening (no matter how hard they scream). Performers are encouraged to explore the act of trying to speak out, in a world that is intent on not listening.

– at the end of a line indicates a sentence that is interrupted or continued by another character.

1.

Bedroom.

Janet   Last night he came to me.
As God is my witness,
He knocked on my door.

Lying in bed,
I heard his ghost call my name.

Ghost appears.

Hello?

2.

Limbo.

Janet   Stephen?

Lee   Kevin?

Carole   Chris?

3.

Otherworld.

Lights flicker.

Resident   Yeah, well,
When it was built,
Us locals got a letter.
An invitation to see
A high-security prison,

19

Wings with three floors,
CCTV.

Eight hundred men,
Eight hundred pairs of feet,
Eight hundred incarcerated souls.
Coming here,
To Milton Keynes.

All this capital,
All this effort,
All this human energy.

For a box of souls on our front door.

4.

Limbo.

Janet   I didn't

Lee   Always walk

Carole   This lonely road

5.

Club.

Lee   Fifteen,
                The noise,
                I was doing cloakroom.

Janet   Scumbag,
                I'm just a working class,
                Council house scumbag.

Lee   Sixteen,
                The bassline,
                Glass collector.

Carole	As kids, We'd pile our teddies and toys, Put them on the bed.
Lee	Seventeen, The rave, Lost in the crowd.
	In the club, I wasn't me. I was not Lee.
	I was one with music, On the jungle scene.

6.

Limbo.

Janet	Voiceless
Lee	On this
Carole	Lonely road

7.

Club.

Lee	Dad remarried, The beat goes on.
Janet	I woke up, sick as a dog.
	Took a test, Pregnant, Shit.
	Stephen was a breech birth. He came into the world folded, Arse first.

Lee	I got a stepbrother, The beat goes on.
Carole	On the bed, our sailing ship. We would hold on. My brother Chris and me, Teddies, toys, All trying not to drown.
Lee	Kevin was a rule breaker. The beat, The beat, The beat goes on.

8.

Limbo.

Janet	My son
Lee	My stepbrother
Carole	My brother

9.

Club.

Janet	I love
Lee	Saying
Carole	His name

10.

Limbo.

Janet	Keeps

| Lee | Him |
| Carole | Alive |

11.

Club.

Janet	Stephen
Lee	Kevin
Carole	Chris

Ghost appears.

12.

Limbo.

Janet	The beat goes on
Lee	The beat goes on
Carole	The beat goes on and on and on

13.

Otherworld.

Lights flicker.

Prison Officer	Hit record. Yeah, that's fine.
Zoom	Recording in progress.
Prison Officer	Every day as a prison officer In Milton Keynes is the same.

Unlock the same doors,
Count the same people,
Walk around clockwise,
Walk anti-clockwise.

Do the same things,
Say the same things.

Every minute,
Every hour,
Every day, the same.

Prison's like a revolving door.
In and out,
Round and round.

How many lads who left this prison
Ended up somewhere worse?
Or dead?

Zoom   Recording stopped.

Prison Officer I think the answer is probably too many.

14.

School.

Carole   Wherever Chris walked,
                    Trouble followed.

                    Beat up and bullied.
                    Boys at school, they just didn't get
                    How gentle and caring
                    My brother could be.

Lee   GCSEs and college
                    Just really weren't for me.

                    I got a job in a warehouse
                    On the edge of Milton Keynes.

	Kevin would sometimes bunk school. He had these wild ambitions and dreams.
Janet	It was just me, Stephen and sod all money.
	I cycled miles to clean at Eton College. Come home, cook dinner, Then do six till midnight shelf-stacking.

15.

Limbo.

| Ghost | David Hunter |

Seeds scatter.

16.

School.

Carole	After school, My brother would walk Head down.
	Just like with his Hood up.
	Lost in his music, Earphones on.
Lee	Head in the stars, Kevin had ambitions and dreams.
	Bigger than our school, Bigger than our estate, Bigger than Milton Keynes.

Janet	A choir boy, a rugby player,
	Stephen, he grew.
	While I cycled miles.

Took a test,
Pregnant again,
Shit.

I didn't know I was expecting twins
Until my twenty-week scan.

17.

Limbo.

Ghost   Sean Brock

Seeds scatter.

18.

School.

| **Carole** | Wherever Chris walked, |
| | Trouble followed. |

Mum and Dad split.
Chris went with Dad.

My brother started drinking,
Going missing.

Lee	Kevin's school,
	They knocked it down.
	All of it is levelled now.
	Like all those ambitions and dreams.

Janet	For Christmas
	I bought Stephen and the twins
	Bob Marley T-shirts.

Stephen,
Nathan and Aaron.
My three little birds.

19.

Limbo.

Ghost   Dwane Harper

Seeds scatter.

20.

Otherworld.

Lights flicker.

Prison Service This call is from a person
Currently in'a prison.
Calls are logged and recorded
And may be listened to by
A member of prison staff.
If you do not wish to accept this call,
Please hang up now.

A3745JF   You get a number,
You're not a name.

A2001RN   I made a mistake,
Ended up here.

A3745JF   I arrived in Milton Keynes in a prison van,
The sweatbox.

A2001RN   This prison has a history,
It has a past.

A3745JF   Strip search.

A2001RN	It's a big jail,
	Concrete walkways.
	Painted on one wall is a black sheep.
	Like every family has a black sheep.
A3745JF	Photograph.
A2001RN	A lot of people can't handle it.
	On their first night they
	Bang,
	Bang,
	Bang,
	On their cell door.
A3745JF	See healthcare.
A2001RN	This one guy was an electrician,
	First time inside.
	He stripped out the wire in his cell,
	Wrapped it around his body
	And put his feet in water.
A3745JF	Prison issue toothbrush.
A2001RN	A slow death.
	Took all night.
A3745JF	You get a number,
	You're not a name.
A2001RN	They fumigated his cell,
	But you could still smell him on the wing
	For days.
A3745JF	Now,
	You're just a number.
A2001RN	A2001RN.
A3745JF	A3745JF.

21.

Limbo.

Janet	Too
Lee	Many
Carole	Regrets

22.

Car.

Janet   Pack up and drive.

Neighbours always
Knocking,
Knocking,
Knocking,
On my door.

Like,
'Your Stephen's done this,'
Or,
'Janet, the twins have done that.'

So we would just pack up and drive.

Lee   I signed on the dotted line
For Queen and Country.

It was my passing out parade
When what happened, happened.
It happened in an Aldi car park.

Carole   I was just like watching telly,
When I got a phone call.
They said,
'Your brother is on top of a building.'

23.

Limbo.

Ghost   Jonathan White

Seeds scatter.

24.

Car.

Janet   Pack up,
                   Took a test.
                   Pregnant,
                   Sophia, a gift.

                   Drive.
                   The boys were so loving.
                   I used to look at them,
                   Holding their baby sister.

                   Pack up and drive.
                   A girl and three boys
                   With special educational needs.
                   I couldn't cope.

Lee   Police found a body in an Aldi car park.

Carole   'Your brother is on top of a building.
                   Can you come now?'

25.

Limbo.

Janet   Just

Lee   Hold

Carole   On

26.

Car.

Janet	Pack up,
	What if I lose my temper,
	Do something I regret?
	Drive,
	I was scared of myself.
	Most nights I'd down a bottle of wine,
	Get blooted, job done.
	Pack up and drive.
	My three little birds
	And Sophia,
	They could feel it, you know?
Lee	I watched Kevin change.
	Ever since the day
	Police found a body in an Aldi car park.
Carole	'Your brother is on top of a building,
	Can you come now?'
	I ran to the car.
	'Jump,
	He's gonna jump.'

27.

Otherworld.

Lights flicker.

Nurse 1	Hi,
	Sorry about the noise.
	I'm just getting my MOT done,
	I thought I'd give you a try.

Nurse 2	My first job was at Burger King. I did a day and quit. My second job was in prison healthcare In Milton Keynes.
Nurse 1	Hi, Sorry, can you –
Nurse 3	One lad, When I was working in healthcare, Had the mental age of seven. The officers used to bring him Colouring books.
Nurse 1	Are you there?
Nurse 3	But when government after government Cut and shut mental health units, Where else was this lad going to go?
Nurse 1	Can you hear me?
Nurse 2	We spent so long trying To keep the men safe from each other, We forgot to keep the men Safe from themselves.
Nurse 1	Yeah, I can hear you –
Nurse 2	No clinical supervision, No suicide prevention training, In healthcare we got nothing at all.
Nurse 1	Right, okay –
Nurse 3	Men with mental illness, Men with addiction, Men with childhood trauma. Where do we expect them to go?
Nurse 1	So, I was one of the nurses –

Nurse 3	Prison is where they go.
Nurse 1	Your first time in prison is so hard.
	This guy I was treating
	Was already so, so damaged.

Hallucinating,
This guy barricaded himself in his cell.
Tried to hang himself.
Survived five days, then died.

I couldn't sleep.
Every time I closed my eyes,
I saw that guy.

Sorry,
Can I call you back?
I think my car's ready.

28.

Porch.

Lee	Back home on leave,
	And Kevin had become a troubled boy.

Kevin's dad.
Police found my stepbrother's dad
In an Aldi car park.

Carole	I talked Chris down,
	Drove him home.
	My brother told me
	He'd been living on the streets.

Doctors diagnosed him with
Agoraphobia,
Paranoia,
Borderline personality disorder.

	'If I didn't have you, Carole, I'd be fucked.' That's what Chris would say.
Lee	Bosnia. Infantry, Royal Green Jackets.
Janet	Out the front door, Stephen was never home.
	Always on the rugby field, Six foot and strong. My son could run and run.
	No one could stop him On the run.

29.

Limbo.

Ghost	Daniel Byrne

Seeds scatter.

30.

Porch.

Lee	Back home on leave, Kevin was self-medicating. Gone was the boy With ambitions and dreams.
	Kevin owed money to a gang in Luton, For all the heroin.
Carole	Chris hated how much things had changed. I had a family,

	A job in a school, Children of my own.

Eight cans a day,
My brother was a drinker.
He said he liked living alone.

I did his shopping,
Checked in on Chris once a week.
I tried and tried
To stop us all from drowning.

Lee   Northern Ireland.
Driver, Royal Logistics Corps.

Janet   Out the front door,
Stephen was never home.

Shoplifting,
Smoking weed,
Excluded from school.

No one could stop him,
On the run.

31.

Limbo.

Ghost   Ryan Harvey

Seeds scatter.

32.

Porch.

Lee   Back home on leave,
Kevin was banged up for armed robbery.
He was in too deep.

Carole	Chris phoned the hospital, Said he was going to hurt himself. Police found him at home With a knife in his hand. They tossed him in jail.
Lee	Sandhurst. A private, Royal Logistics Corps.
Janet	Out the front door, Stephen didn't come home. Police caught him on the run.
	In the visitor waiting room I bought my son some Starburst.
	Stephen liked Starburst.

33.

Limbo.

Ghost	Ian Brown

Seeds scatter.

34.

Porch.

Lee	The prison is a stone's throw away From our house.
Carole	Chris had a bed, He was being fed, I thought he was safe.
Lee	Nearly everyone on my estate Has been there.

Janet	In the car park,
	Outside the visitor waiting room,
	There was a sign.

Lee	Everyone in Milton Keynes
	Knows about what happens at –

All	Woodhill.

35.

Otherworld.

Lights flicker.

A dog barks.

Victim Support Worker	Age fifteen,
	I was the victim of a crime.
	Stranger danger, not very nice.
	Now I'm a victim support worker.

Magistrate	I became a magistrate a few months ago.
	It's quite a depressing retirement project,
	Sometimes.

But it's also fascinating and rewarding.
Sometimes you end up with people
Failed by the system in all kinds of ways.

Sometimes,
Not all of the time.

Volunteer	Hello,
	Yes, so at the Winter Night Shelter
	We see a lot of ex-offenders.

They come in.
Tea,
Coffee,

	Breakfast,
	Shower and gather their thoughts.

Magistrate   The judicial system is like a hallway
With lots of doors.
At each stage of the judicial process,
You can exit.

A dog barks.

Victim Support Worker   As a victim,
Once your case has gone to court,
You're legally bound to testify
Whether you want to or not.

You'll be breaking the law
If you back out now.

The ultimate goal is justice
But does this system
Make us feel any better?

Magistrate   Open a door,
Case dismissed, you can exit.
Can't get out?
Down the hall you go.

Volunteer   Milton Keynes
Is a hard city to be homeless in.
This one guy came to us,
He'd been sleeping in the underpass
With literally nothing.

He was like,
'It's so cold,
I'm going to reoffend and go back.
Back to Woodhill.'

Magistrate   Open a door,
Community order, you can exit.
Can't get out?
Down the hall you go.

Victim Support Worker   I see myself in the victims
I support in the witness box.
But I also just want to leap over
To those lads who testify,
You know?

Lads,
Who've not had equal access to care.

Lads,
Who've not had equal access to compassion.

Lads,
Who've not had equal access to love.

Magistrate   Down and down the hall you go.
Deeper and further into the system.
Until you run out of doors.

Volunteer   At the shelter,
We lose contact with so many men.
But suddenly they come back to us again,
Back through our doors.

Magistrate   Centuries ago,
If you ran out of doors,
You could find yourself
At the end of the gallows.

What do you think happens
To people today?
The ones who run out of doors.

Victim Support Worker   Age fifteen,
I was the victim of a crime.
Stranger danger, not very nice.
I never had my day in court.
And you know,
I'm so glad I never did.

A dog barks.

I'm sorry,
He's a German Shepherd.
That's why he barks so loud.

36.

Limbo.

Janet   Couldn't

Lee   Reach

Carole   Him

37.

Church.

Carole   Pray,
             Chris couldn't carry my dad's coffin.

             Pray,
             My brother was cuffed to an officer
             The whole time.

             Pray,
             Chris just lost it,
             Howled the church down.

All   Let us pray.

Lee   I quit the army.
             Came home,
             Moved in with my partner Lynsey.

             Doctors were telling me
             Kevin had bipolar disorder.
             He'd been diagnosed with schizophrenia.

	We had to get him out, Out of Woodhill.
All	Let us pray.
Janet	In and out, Stephen was released from prison.
	He couldn't get a job, Not with a criminal record. Job after job turned my son away.
	Didn't like it inside, Didn't like it out.
	Stephen was lost, Totally lost.

38.

Limbo.

| **Ghost** | Joanna Latham |

Seeds scatter.

39.

Church.

Carole	My brother's eyes, Amen, Had changed.
	His eyes, Amen, Looked dead.
	Dead, Amen, Totally dead.

41

All	Let us pray.
Lee	Doctors were telling me Kevin was a regular self-harmer. They should have sectioned him Months before his arrest.
	We had to get him out, Out of Woodhill.
All	Let us pray.
Janet	In and out The bloody pawn shop
	Stephen and the twins Pawned my DVDs, my TV.
	My three little birds Used the money for drugs.

40.

Limbo.

Janet	Couldn't
Lee	Pull
Carole	Him out

41.

Church.

Carole	Arms linked I felt my brother break.
	At the end of the service, The officer took Chris back to Woodhill.

All	Let us pray.
Lee	Doctors were telling me Kevin needed a mental health bed, Not prison.
	We needed to get him out. Out, Out, Out of Woodhill.
All	Let us pray.
Janet	In and out Of each other's lives.
	Stephen and me drifted, I couldn't do it anymore.
	Drinking became more of a habit, What with all my worries.
	Stephen and me weren't speaking When he got sent back to prison. Back to Woodhill.

42.

Otherworld.

Lights flicker.

Chaplain	At Woodhill, It didn't matter At what time of day or what time of night. You could be called to accompany A family liaison officer To break the news of a death. They'd pop you in a taxi and off you go.

43

You knock on the door
And as soon as the family sees the uniform,
They know.
So you're gentle but clear.
'Sorry, it isn't good news.'

And you step inside knowing full well
That you're about to put a bomb
Under somebody's life.

43.

Living room.

A phone rings.

Carole	I was at my dad's cottage.
Lee	'Hello?'
Carole	Clearing out his stuff.
Janet	'What?'
Carole	When I got a call.

44.

Otherworld.

Lights flicker.

Chris's Mum   My son.

45.

Living room.

A phone rings.

Carole   I was like,
                    'Mum?'

46.

Otherworld.
Lights flicker.
Chris's Mum   My son.

47.

Living room.
Carole   'Mum?'

48.

Otherworld.
Lights flicker.
Chris's Mum   My son.

                    Downstairs,
                    I could hear voices.

                    My partner called.
                    'Linda, there's two men here from Woodhill.
                    It's Chris.'

49.

Living room.
Carole   'Mum?'

50.

Otherworld.

Lights flicker.

Chris's Mum In the lounge, on the settee,
These two men, so cold,
Just came out with it.

'Chris was found unresponsive in his cell.'

51.

Living room.

Carole 'Mum?'

52.

Otherworld.

Lights flicker.

Chris's Mum They were like,
'We travelled all this way
To give you the news.'

And I was like,
'What? Am I supposed to be grateful?'

53.

Living room.

Carole 'Mum!'

54.

Otherworld.

Lights flicker.

Chris's Mum   I'd only spoken to Chris the day before.
He'd only phoned me, the day before.

55.

Living room.

Carole   I was like,
'Mum,
Did you tell Chris?'

56.

Otherworld.

Lights flicker.

Chris's Mum   Chris told me he was scared.

57.

Living room.

Carole   'Mum,
Did you tell Chris?'

58.

Otherworld.

Lights flicker.

Chris's Mum   Chris told me he was being threatened.

59.

Living room.

Carole   'Mum,
                Did you tell Chris?'

60.

Otherworld.

Lights flicker.

Chris's Mum   Chris told me
                    Someone was going to hurt him.

61.

Living room.

Carole   'Mum,
                Did you tell Chris?'

62.

Otherworld.

Lights flicker.

Chris's Mum   Chris told me
                    They were corrupt at Woodhill.

63.

Living room.

Carole   'Mum?
               Did you tell Chris that I love him?'

64.

Otherworld.

Lights flicker.

Chris's Mum   And then,
                    The line went dead.

65.

Living room.

Janet   My whole world

Lee   Turned upside down.

Carole   Now I dance

All   In the horror of grief.

They end the call.

66.

Limbo.

Ghost   This is an investigation
              Into the death of a man,
              Who has been found dead in his cell
              At HMP Woodhill.

I offer my condolences
To his family and friends.

67.

Otherworld.

Lights flicker.

Academic	My take? Prison is basically An admission of social policy failure. Locking people up should be a last resort.
	And I mean, Maybe I'm a starry-eyed academic. But change can happen. It's just nobody listens and nobody cares.
Architect	Please do tell me when to stop, Because I don't want to be known As that bloody architect whining on. But like, What is prison truly for?
Academic	Centuries ago, Prison officers put your hand in a crank And tightened the screw. Grind people good, That was the idea.
Architect	Yeah, well I mean, Victorians designed small prison cells With a high window.
	The idea was you'd look up, Like the view from an altar, See the image of God and repent.

Modern prison design
Is a hangover from that.

A cell no bigger than a cupboard.
A cocooning,
A removal of somebody
From everyone and everything.

Academic   Woodhill is a high security prison.
It has a close supervision unit
And it's a local prison.
If you are looking for conditions
To create a disaster,
There you are.

Architect   A connective tissue runs between
Prisons and social housing estates.

Both built by materials
That are cheap and durable.

Designed by someone
Who will never live there.

A guy in prison once told me,
'This place is like my old council estate.
I feel like I've been prepared for this place
My whole life.'

Academic   It is impossible to understate
The impact of cutbacks.
Nobody listened.

Everybody knew there were no longer
Enough prison staff at Woodhill.
Nobody cared.

The size of our prison population
Is rising and rising.
Nobody listened, nobody cared.

Architect	Well I mean, The whole justice system Is built, Is designed, Is architectured, To make your heart quiver. Power lies with someone who sits up high, While you must sit below.
Academic	It isn't a surprise, right? What happens at Woodhill. It was coming. What did we do about it? Jack shit.

68.

Limbo.

Janet	I wake up
Lee	And
Carole	He is there

69.

Inquest.

Ghost	I remind you no one is on trial.
Janet	The prison called, they said, 'Do you want to go and see Your son's body? He's in Milton Keynes Hospital.'

	Stephen had been in cold storage But he looked so peaceful. I took photographs.
	I know that sounds morbid or whatever, But I took photographs.
Ghost	There is no prosecution or defence.
Lee	All these papers arrived. Out of order, Upside down, Back to front, Proper information dump.
	I don't read or write that well, But I sat up all night highlighting bits. Reading it all, The way Kevin died.
Ghost	There is no quest for liability.
Carole	The prison brought my brother's belongings In a cardboard box.
	A T-shirt, A piece of paper, And a pair of white trainers.
	Chris went into Woodhill with red trainers So, whose are these?

70.

Limbo.

| **Ghost** | Simon Turvey |

Leaves scatter.

71.

Inquest.

Carole	It took a year For the inquest to happen.
Ghost	You must answer four questions.
Lee	Waiting, With so many questions.
Ghost	One, Who died?
Janet	Waiting for answers.
Ghost	Two, When did he die?
Janet	My son is dead And all I have left are photographs.
Ghost	Three, Where did he die?
Lee	All I have left are papers.
Ghost	Four, How did he die?
Carole	All I have left is this cardboard box.
All	That's all I have left.

72.

Limbo.

Janet	I go to sleep
Lee	And
Carole	He is there

73.

Otherworld.

Lights flicker.

Lord	The Ministry of Justice Needed to demonstrate They were doing something About the deaths.
	So, They approached me As a member of the House of Lords And said, 'Will you do this review Into children and young adults Who died in prison?'
	Cappuccino please.
Minister	When I was Prison Minister, I used to have nightmares. You know, About me being a prisoner.
Lord	When there is a death in prison There is an inquest for families. I met so many.
	This is supposed to be your opportunity To hear what happened, To learn who's responsible.
	Normal milk is fine.
Minister	Nightmares, About being in a cell. Locked in with no power.
Lord	Families find themselves In a small waiting room

With the lawyers representing the prison.
Representing the people who they feel
Killed their child.

Have in, please.

Minister   Nightmares,
Where everything you've assumed about life
Is gone.

Lord   I gave my advice:

Prison
Is an expensive failure.

Prison
Does not rehabilitate or intervene.

Prison
Fails to ask,
'Why are so many young adults even here
in the first place?'

Card please.

Minister   So many nightmares.

But you know,
I'm still a public protection kind of guy.

You should sacrifice your liberty,
You should lose your vote,
There needs to be punishment.

Lord   I gave my advice.
Children and young adults
Spend hours alone in a cell
With nothing to do.

Other than stare at a light fitting.
Then stare at their bedding,
Or belt,
Or shoelaces.

Minister	I sound like I'm wringing my hands But I don't think You'll ever stop death in prison. I don't think you're ever going To stop the death.
Lord	I gave my advice and did they listen? That's everything, thank you.

74.

Inquest.

All	Jury in.
Carole	The inquest is a blur. Prison officers testified, All sticking to a script.
Ghost	Drugs.
Carole	They said –
Ghost	Chris was smoking drugs –
Carole	In his cell.
All	Swear them in.
Lee	My stepbrother was self-harming.
Ghost	Cuts and cigarette burns –
Lee	All down his arms.
Ghost	Low.
Lee	Prison officers considered Kevin's risk of self-harm to be low.
All	Next witness.
Janet	A note appeared in evidence –

Ghost	'I can't sleep.'
Janet	A note from my son –
Ghost	'Constant thoughts are running, Running through my mind.'
Janet	A note to prison healthcare –
Ghost	'I've cut my arms, It takes the pressure away.'
Janet	Why did nobody do anything?
All	Adjourn.

75.

Limbo.

Ghost	Ireneusz Połubiński

Leaves scatter.

76.

Inquest.

All	Jury in.
Carole	Prison officers testified Like cogs in a machine.
Ghost	Debt.
Carole	They said my brother was in –
Ghost	Drug debt.
Carole	Wherever Chris walked, Debt, it followed.
All	Swear them in.

Lee	My stepbrother took –
Ghost	Thirty naproxen And one hundred paracetamol, All in one go.
Lee	Staff didn't take him to hospital.
Ghost	Low.
Lee	Prison officers considered Kevin's risk of self-harm to be low.
All	Next witness.
Janet	Another note appeared in evidence –
Ghost	'I'm going to set fire to my cell, Just watch me.'
Janet	Another note from my son –
Ghost	'I'm going to get out of this jail, Just watch me.'
Janet	Why did nobody do anything?
All	Adjourn.

77.

Limbo.

Ghost	Robert Fenlon

Leaves scatter.

78.

Inquest.

All	Jury in.

Carole	Prison officers testified, Like this just happens every day.
Ghost	Threatened.
Carole	They were like –
Ghost	Chris was threatened with a blade.
Carole	To pay his drug debts.
All	Swear them in.
Lee	Kevin was self-harming.
Ghost	He was given a warning For disruptive and aggressive behaviour.
Lee	My stepbrother was just left –
Ghost	Alone in a cell
Lee	For twenty-two hours a day.
Ghost	Low.
Lee	Prison officers considered Kevin's risk of self-harm to be low.
All	Next witness.
Janet	At the end of the first day of the inquest –
All	Adjourn.
Janet	We were told –
Ghost	'This morning, Another man has been found dead At Woodhill.'
Janet	I called the twins, Nathan and Aaron. But they didn't pick up.

I needed Stephen,
I needed the twins,
I needed my three little birds.
And Sophia, my gift.

79.

Limbo.

Ghost   Michael Cameron

Leaves scatter.

80.

Otherworld.

Lights flicker.

Inspector   Let me put a light on
                   So you can bloody see me.

                   Right,
                   Imagine being in a cell.

                   Somebody hands you a book
                   A little box to stand on.

                   Up
                   On your box, you can see light.

                   Another book,
                   Up.
                   On your boxes, you can see tops of trees.

                   Another book,
                   Up.
                   Definite daylight.

Another book,
Up.
You can see the whole horizon.

You can see a way out.

Family Liaison Officer   This is quite tricky.
I was a family liaison officer.
There's history, okay?

My first few years
At Woodhill were uneventful
But then things began to escalate, rather.

One person took their life, then another.
Like a contagion.

Inspector   Another book,
Up.

Visitor   Yeah, honestly like,
I was a prison visitor at Woodhill.
I visited so many boys.

Boys,
Who'd been excluded from school.

Boys,
In prison often because
Wrong place, wrong time.

Lonely boys,
Who would always ask,
'Come visit again?'

No way out.

Inspector   Another book,
Up.

Family Liaison Officer   Why do people
Take their lives in prison?
Well, that's the six-million-dollar question.
A way out.

Inspector	Another book,
	Up.
Visitor	School is a protector,
	It keeps children safe.
	But in that visitor room,
	I saw forgotten boys.
	All excluded.
	Fallen through the cracks.
	Boys,
	Who weren't getting out.
Inspector	Another book,
	Up.
Family Liaison Officer	On my last day at Woodhill,
	I drove away kind of numb, really.
	It's brutal for everybody
	And that's the way it is.
	Did efficiency savings
	Precipitate prison deaths?
	I got out.
Inspector	Another book,
	Up.
Visitor	I saw boys,
	Given no chance of redemption.
	Boys,
	Excluded from a school
	By teachers that are white.
	Boys,
	Sentenced by a judge that is white.
	Boys,
	I visited so many Black boys
	With no way out.

Inspector	Another book, Up.
	I did some prison inspector work. I saw an awful lot of men, Never given a chance to read or write.
	I saw a prison Stop a man doing his A-levels Because it took a bit of effort On the prison side.
	I saw this government Ban books for men inside.
	Imagine getting a book, A little box to stand on And it's taken away?
	Imagine never getting a book at all?
	Your whole horizon goes dark. And taken away is your way out.

81.

Limbo.

Janet	Swallow
Lee	The
Carole	Pain

82.

Inquest.

Ghost	'Can you hear me?'

Lee	March 12th, Officers discovered two razor blades Under Kevin's pillow.
Ghost	'I'd love to kill myself.'
Lee	March 13th Officers found Kevin With a ligature around his neck.
Ghost	'I think about cutting ten times a day. Gives me a buzz.'
Lee	March 29th Officers picked up a note Under Kevin's cell door.
Ghost	'I want to go.'
Lee	Officers knew About my stepbrother's Dark ambitions and dreams. They fucking knew.

83.

Limbo.

Ghost	Thomas Morris

Leaves scatter.

84.

Inquest.

Ghost	In our healthcare assessment, Stephen made good eye contact.
Janet	Witnesses mumble.

Ghost	In our healthcare assessment, Stephen had good body language.
Janet	Lawyers' papers shuffle.
Ghost	In our healthcare assessment, Stephen reported a long history Of suicide attempts.
Janet	'But he's fine now.' That's what their assessment said.
Ghost	Our investigator Has been unable to discover Who wrote that assessment entry.
Janet	What?

85.

Limbo.

Janet	Bottle
Lee	Up
Carole	The grief

86.

Inquest.

Ghost	No,
Carole	Chris locked himself in his cell. He didn't come out for weeks.
Ghost	No action was taken.
Carole	Chris was going hungry, Petrified.

Ghost	No,
Carole	Men were gathering Outside my brother's cell door.
Ghost	No action was taken.
Carole	Men gathering to collect their debt.
Ghost	No,
Carole	Prison officers knew The names of all the drug dealers.
Ghost	No action was taken.
Carole	Prison officers knew Because Chris gave them the names.
Ghost	No, No action was taken.
Carole	Why didn't officers stop the dealers? We hadn't opened up a can of worms here.
All	This was a barrel of worms.

87.

Otherworld.

Lights flicker.

Dealer	Alright then, Hit record, let's go.
Governor	I've sort of travelled through blood, You know what I mean? Been a prison governor, Got the T-shirt.
Dealer	My husband went into Woodhill clean And came out with a raging heroin habit.

Governor	Corruption, like love, is all around. Mobile phones, Drugs, Large cartons of orange juice. Prison officers have smuggled it all, For the right price.
Dealer	I was coaxed into it. My husband made me get my hands dirty. I would buy drugs and drop them off. Sometimes it was a garden, Sometimes it was a supermarket toilet, Sometimes it was a flower pot Outside a primary school. A screw, an officer, Would pick up the drugs. Take them into Woodhill.
Governor	One governor gave prisoners Biscuits and cans of Red Bull for Sex in the prison library. Presents from the Argos catalogue For sexual favours.
Dealer	Prison is a big fucking game. Who has the best designer clothes? Who has kitted out their cell? Who has the power?
Governor	Anti-corruption and keep prisoners alive, That's the job now really.
Dealer	If you have drugs, You're going to smash prison.
Governor	We refuse to see, What happens behind the prison wall.

	We refuse to see, The lives being wasted.
	We refuse to see, This nation's addiction To locking people up.
	At this rate, We will incarcerate ourselves to death.
Dealer	I served my time as a dealer. I fucking regret it, of course I do.
	But sometimes the only difference Between the person sitting in the cell And the person locking the cell, Is that one of them is wearing a uniform. Do you get me?
	Right, time's up. I've gotta go.

88.

Inquest.

Carole	The courtroom only had one door. Prison officers were always hanging around That one door.
	Every morning, Pushing my way through, The men who killed my brother.
	The night before he died, Chris told Mum –
Ghost	'It's hell in here. When I sleep, I dream I am chopping carrots With the Grim Reaper.'

69

Carole	In pieces, My brother was on the phone like –
Ghost	'When I sleep, Mum, I dream of death.'
Carole	Wherever Chris walked, Death, it followed.
Ghost	'When I sleep, Mum, I dream I dine with death.'
Lee	The morning he died, My stepbrother spat on a prison officer.
Ghost	'Smash it all up.'
Lee	Kevin was facing an indeterminate sentence, Imprisonment for public protection.
Ghost	'If I get that, I'll do myself in.'
Lee	Lock him up with no release date, Throw away the key.
Ghost	'My head can't take it.'
Janet	Hours before he died, Stephen sat in his cell.
Ghost	'I'm going to get out of this jail, Just watch me.'
Janet	Head in his hands, My son, he sat alone in the dark.
All	'Just you watch me.'

89.

Limbo.

Ghost	Daniel Dunkley

Leaves scatter.

90.

Inquest.

Carole	That night, Chris told Mum
Ghost	'I need to get out.'
Carole	They found pieces of paper In my brother's cell.
Ghost	'Out.'
Carole	Written down were mobile numbers, Bank details.
Ghost	'I need to get out.'
Carole	Debt, Pages and pages of prison debt. Nobody investigated.
Ghost	'Out.'
Carole	Chris got hold of a load of Prescription medication and drugs. He took them all.
All	'I need to get out.'
Lee	Kevin waited till lunchtime.
Ghost	'Help.'
Lee	A guard always unlocked Kevin at lunchtime.
Ghost	'Can you help me?'

Lee	My stepbrother bet his life An officer would unlock him at lunchtime.
Ghost	'Help.'
Lee	Kevin tied a bed sheet, round the top bunk And in a cry for help, He jumped.
Ghost	'Can you help me?'
Lee	But that day, The officer was running ten minutes behind.
All	'Help, Can anyone help me?'
Janet	Stephen pressed the emergency bell.
Ghost	'This place' –
Janet	Then hung himself in his cell.
Ghost	'Is killing me.'
Janet	My son prayed someone would come.
Ghost	'This place' –
Janet	But nobody did.
Ghost	'Is killing me.'
Janet	Nobody came.
All	'Killing me, This place is killing me.'

91.

Limbo.

Ghost	Jason Basalat

Leaves scatter.

92.

Inquest.

Carole	Officers found Chris, In a pool of his own vomit.
All	Cold to the touch.
Lee	Officers found Kevin, Lying at the end of his cell.
All	No pulse.
Janet	Officers found Stephen, Swinging in the dark.
All	No signs of life.
Carole	An overdose.
All	'No, We didn't call code blue.'
Lee	A bed sheet.
All	'No, We didn't call code blue.'
Janet	A swinging shadow.
All	'No, We didn't call code blue.'

93.

Limbo.

Ghost	Brett Olerich

Leaves scatter.

94.

Otherworld.

Lights flicker.

National Chairman   Hi,
Yeah, I'm lost.
Where should I go?

Investigator   Woodhill has been defined by its failures.
I was commissioned
By the Ministry of Justice
To report on self-inflicted deaths.

I conducted
Focused observations in reception
Which coincided with acute staff shortages.
I required a snapshot of the prison.

Education Tutor   It ripples,
Let me tell you.
I was an education tutor at Woodhill
And when someone dies, it ripples.

Investigator   Prisoner A,
Spoke very little English.

Prisoner B,
History of self-harm.

National Chairman   So,
Violence doesn't bother me.

Unemployment,
Riots,
Managed decline.

I was raised in violence,
Surrounded by it.

Investigator   Prisoner C,
Short sentence.

                        Prisoner D,
                        Depressive illness, problem with alcohol.

National Chairman   I was a labourer
                        On a building site in Liverpool.
                        Saw these adverts
                        To become a prison officer.
                        Doubled my wages overnight.

                        I was accused of assault by a prisoner.
                        My union protected me.
                        I wanted to give something back.

                        Now I chair a union.
                        I speak out for prison officers.

Investigator   Prisoner E,
                        Desperate for a smokers pack.

                        Prisoner F,
                        Self-harmed in court.

Education Tutor   A death is so hard for prison staff.
                        You can't sleep.
                        Just dark thoughts,
                        Running through your mind.

                        What did I miss?
                        Could I have done anything else?
                        It ripples.

Investigator   Prisoner G,
                        Did not sleep well.

                        Prisoner H,
                        History of drug abuse.

National Chairman   Cutbacks mean,
                        Prisoners only get half an hour unlock,
                        Then they're banged up again.
                        It's the only way to keep everybody safe.

Investigator   Two hours at reception.

Education Tutor   The irony is,
It was Men's Mental Health Day
When it happened.

Lucas was a personal trainer.
He was tall and strong.

Lucas was always making jokes,
Always up for a laugh.

Lucas was always the first port of call
To cut a prisoner down.

Investigator   Prisoner I,
Detoxing.

Prisoner J,
Suffered from depression.

Education Tutor   Lucas bottled it up,
And then took his own life.

Devastating, yeah.
The ripple.

Investigator   Prisoner K,
First time in prison, on remand.

Prisoner L,
Disciplinary charge for cannabis.

National Chairman   Cutbacks mean,
One officer on a wing.
And cell bells are going off
All over the place.

What can wait ten minutes?
Will my boss be here soon?
Which cell do I pick?

It's so sad if you pick the wrong one.

Investigator	Prisoner M,
	Said the judge made a mistake.
	Prisoner N,
	Some bravado.
Education Tutor	What's tragic
	Is that it becomes normalised.
	In prison,
	You come to accept the ripple.
Investigator	Prisoner O,
	Returned from court.
National Chairman	Cutbacks mean prisons are failing.
	A system
	That doesn't heed the warning signs.
	A system
	Of managed decline.
Investigator	Staff were run ragged at Woodhill.
	Everyone was frightened of being
	The next one in court.
	After two hours of focused observations,
	I was told by staff
	'Our job at night is to try and keep
	Prisoners alive.'

95.

Limbo.

Janet	All the time
Lee	I think about
Carole	His last moments

96.

Inquest.

Janet	Officers cut my son down, They laid Stephen on the floor.
Ghost	No radio to summon for help.
Janet	Officers said there was no heartbeat.
Ghost	Our first aid certificates had both expired.
Janet	Too late.
Ghost	Resuscitation attempts unsuccessful.
All	The man was declared dead.

97.

Limbo.

Janet	All the time
Lee	I think about
Carole	His last thoughts

98.

Inquest.

Lee	Fifteen minutes, Kevin was lying there While officers floundered.
Ghost	I radioed for the nurse.
Lee	Fifteen minutes, No one did first aid.

Ghost	I was waiting for the nurse.
Lee	Fifteen minutes, No one called an ambulance.
Ghost	No heartbeat at all.
All	The man was declared dead.

99.

Limbo.

Janet	All the time
Lee	I think about
Carole	His last wishes

100.

Inquest.

Carole	Four times.
Ghost	It was the nurse.
Carole	Not once.
Ghost	The nurse didn't have any equipment.
Carole	Not twice.
Ghost	Nurses normally bring oxygen, But she didn't have any.
Carole	Not three times.
Ghost	We started CPR.
Carole	Four times. My brother told staff he feared for his life.

| Ghost | Absolutely cold. |
| **All** | The man was declared dead. |

101.

Limbo.

Janet	All the time
Lee	I think about
Carole	His last breath

102.

Inquest.

Janet   Gone.
One of my three little birds was gone.

My son,
My son,
My son.

103.

Otherworld.

Lights flicker.

Daughter   Mum?

104.

Limbo.

Janet   My daughter?

105.

Otherworld.
Lights flicker.
Daughter   Mum?

106.

Limbo.
Janet   Sophia?

107.

Otherworld.
Lights flicker.
Daughter   Mum?

I know we haven't really spoken about
Stephen.
It's so hard.

He was my brother,
Do you know what I mean?

108.

Limbo.
Janet   Sophia, it's okay.

109.

Otherworld.

Lights flicker.

Daughter   Stephen used to come home
At like three in the morning.
He'd literally throw rocks
At my bedroom window.

I'd come downstairs,
Open the back door and let him inside.
I didn't care where he'd been.

He was my big brother.
We just got each other, you know?

110.

Limbo.

Janet   Sophia, I'm here.

111.

Otherworld.

Lights flicker.

Daughter   I didn't write to Stephen in prison.

No,
I was too upset with him.

I was asleep when the phone rang,
When I got the news.

Avoid, avoid, avoid.
Disassociate, autopilot.

I did whatever I could just not to think.

112.

Limbo.

Janet   Sophia!

113.

Otherworld.

Lights flicker.

Daughter   I was just like, why?

                   I wasn't even angry.
                   I was just like,
                   Why?
                   Why?
                   Why?
                   Why did you do that?

114.

Limbo.

Janet   I know.

115.

Otherworld.

Lights flicker.

Daughter   If only
                   I'd written that letter.
                   Then maybe
                   Stephen would still be here.

If only
I'd written that letter.
Then maybe,
Stephen might not have felt so alone.

If only,
I'd written that letter.

116.

Limbo.

Janet   Sophia,
My gift, I'm here.

117.

Otherworld.

Lights flicker.

Daughter I wish,
I'd written that letter.

I wish,
I said sorry for saying things I didn't mean.

I wish,
I'd shown love when I felt it.

I wish,
I'd said I love you.

I wish,
I'd said I'll see you soon.

118.

Limbo.

Janet   Why don't you write it anyway?

119.

Inquest.

Ghost   When reaching your verdict,
                   I remind you.

                   There is no quest for liability.
                   There is no quest for fault in any way.

                   You must answer four questions.

120.

Limbo.

Janet   The inquest
Lee   Just left me
Carole   Numb

121.

Inquest.

Ghost   One,
                   Who died?

122.

Limbo.

Janet	My son
Lee	My stepbrother
Carole	My brother

123.

Inquest.

| Ghost | Two,
When did he die? |

124.

Limbo.

Janet	Four-sixteen p.m.
Lee	One-fifty-five p.m.
Carole	Seven-fifty-five p.m.

125.

Inquest.

| Ghost | Three,
Where did he die? |

126.

Limbo.

| Janet | Cell 302
House Unit 2A
HMP Woodhill |

Lee	Cell 101 House Unit 5 HMP Woodhill
Carole	Cell 310 House Unit 4A HMP Woodhill

127.

Inquest.

Ghost	Four, How did he die?

128.

Limbo.

Janet	My son Did not kill himself
Lee	My stepbrother Did not kill himself
Carole	My brother Did not kill himself

129.

Inquest.

Ghost	If you are reading this letter, I'm sorry.

130.

Limbo.

Janet   Woodhill
               Killed Stephen.

131.

Inquest.

Ghost   I'm sorry.

132.

Limbo.

Lee   Woodhill
               Killed Kevin.

133.

Inquest.

Ghost   I'm sorry

134.

Limbo.

Carole   Woodhill
               Killed Chris.

135.

Inquest.

Ghost   I'm so sorry.

136.

Limbo.

Janet   The state killed my son
Lee   The state killed my stepbrother
Carole   The state killed my brother
All   The state killed our boys

137.

Otherworld.

Lights flicker.

Grendon   I was one of the lucky ones.
                    I got out.

Wandsworth   I am free.

Brixton   I made it out of the human warehouse.

Grendon   On London Bridge,
                    I'd only just been released.
                    Got caught up in an incident.
                    A guy with a knife and bomb.

Wandsworth   Terrified,
                    I hadn't crossed a road in two years.

Brixton   Haunted,
                    Every night I am haunted.

Grendon	On London Bridge, I grabbed the knife. Held the attacker down.
Wandsworth	Bright lights, I had to hold my dad's hand.
Brixton	Haunted by the men Who couldn't fucking hack it.
Grendon	On London Bridge, I looked up. Men in suits were filming.
Wandsworth	I had to hold my dad's hand To cross the road.
Brixton	Haunted by the men left in storage.
Grendon	On London Bridge, I saw men who were free. Filming as police shot the guy dead.
Wandsworth	I left prison And I was too scared to even cross the road.
Brixton	Haunted by the men who died in storage.
Grendon	I got out, But my sentence hangs over me. Those men filming in their suits have liberty. But will I ever really be free?

138.

Kitchen.

Janet	Wine in hand, Slumped on the kitchen counter, I turned myself inside out. Trying to fathom a life without Stephen.

	My flat was piled high With boxes of his stuff.
All	Boxes full of pain.
Lee	I couldn't even go down the shops, Without thinking of Kevin And starting a fight. So I locked myself away.
All	Boxes full of nightmares.
Carole	I hated the world And everyone and everything in it. I didn't tell anyone about Chris.
All	Boxes full of memories of him.

139.

Limbo.

| **Ghost** | David Raynor |

Petals scatter.

140.

Kitchen.

Janet	Another bottle. People say there are five stages of grief. But I couldn't get past stage one.
All	Muddling through paperwork.
Lee	Countless hours of therapy, So many pills. Didn't recognise the man I'd become.

All	Wading through yesterdays.
Carole	I sat on Facebook, Refreshing updates on Woodhill. Scrolling, For nasty comments about my brother.
All	Surrounded by his unfinished life.

141.

Limbo.

Ghost	I tried to be strong for you

142.

Kitchen.

Janet	Another bottle. I carried him, Gave birth to him, Breastfed him. And in such shit circumstances He was taken away.
All	Where do I put the pain?
Lee	My partner Lynsey watched me blow up. Anger became a part of me.
All	Where do I put his dreams?
Carole	I tried to brush thoughts Of my brother away But I'd end up bawling my eyes out. I couldn't escape Chris.
All	Where do I put this grief?

143.

Limbo.

Ghost   Taras Nykolyn

Petals scatter.

144.

Otherworld.

Lights flicker.

Chief Inspectorate   We are yet to reach
                      The bottom of the crisis.
                      My role as Chief Inspectorate
                      Was to monitor whether prisons met
                      International human rights standards.

Ombudsman   Sorry,
                      I'm conscious of the time.

Chief Inspectorate   Why has the prison population
                      Doubled since Maggie Thatcher?
                      Are we twice as dangerous,
                      Or twice as violent?

Ombudsman   Before I retired, I was the
                      Prisons and Probation Ombudsman.
                      Some days it was like
                      Operating a sausage machine.
                      Churning out investigations into deaths.

Chief Inspectorate   What role does populism play?
                      Politicians from all parties
                      Have played on it.
                      Prison sentences are inflating.
                      Men are serving more and more time.

Ombudsman	We were toothless.
	Our ability to follow up recommendations
	Was limited.
	No way of imposing sanctions on prisons.
	No way of enforcing consequences.

Chief Inspectorate	Where do we draw the line?
	We are already
	Building extensions in prisons.
	Building super prisons
	To store thousands of men.

Ombudsman	We were toothless in the sense,
	Death in prison is a cultural issue,
	A systemic issue.
	An issue we were toothless to stop.

145.

Limbo.

Ghost	I'm sorry,
	For all my outbursts

146.

Bus.

Lee	I had to sort my head.
	So, I'd sit at the back of the bus,
	Look out the window and see the stars.

All	Back to work.

Carole	Check my phone at school,
	Facebook ads kept targeting me.
	'Become a prison officer at Woodhill,
	Do something meaningful today.'

All	Back to the grind.
Lee	Anxiety, Depression, PTSD. Who the fuck was going to employ me?
All	Back to life.
Janet	At Eton College, I picked up my old job, cleaning again. Underneath the cobwebs in the scullery, I found bottles and bottles Of Moët Champagne.

147.

Limbo.

Ghost	William Vickers

Petals scatter.

148.

Bus.

Lee	When a star dies, It explodes with such force, It forms a black hole.
All	Keep your head down.
Carole	In the staff room, I was always looking over my shoulder. I lost all trust In the systems and people around me.
All	Keep it together.

Lee	When a star dies,
	It forms a black hole
	With such a gravitational pull,
	Light cannot escape.

| All | Keep pushing on. |

Janet	Underneath the cobwebs in the scullery,
	I began,
	I started to see.
	Life is about the haves and the have-nots.

149.

Limbo.

| Ghost | I'm sorry, |
| | For saying things I should keep to myself. |

150.

Bus.

Lee	When a star dies,
	It forms a black hole
	That pulls everything in.
	It consumes everything,
	It eats the light.

| All | Learn to live with the hurt. |

Carole	After work,
	I'd go straight home.
	My world was shrinking
	Smaller and smaller.

| All | Learn to live with the guilt. |

Lee	When a star dies, Everything dies with it. Everything.
All	Learn to live with the heartache.
Janet	Underneath the cobwebs in the scullery, I saw that my three little birds, My daughter and me, We were the have-nots.
All	Something had to change.

151.

Otherworld.

Lights flicker.

Dad	Monday, My son got stabbed at school.
Police Officer	My husband said I changed Whenever I put the police uniform on.
Dad	Tuesday, My son came home, all stitched up.
Council Worker	I was driving. When the notifications flooded in.
Police Officer	Policing was like shooting fish in a barrel. Gangs hung around pupil referral units. Picking up kids from broken homes in Milton Keynes.
Dad	Wednesday, Police didn't investigate.
Council Worker	I pulled over and opened my phone. A cold sensation went through my body.

Police Officer	One night, I responded to calls of a ten-year-old girl Holding firearms for a gang in London.
Dad	Thursday, Government didn't care What was happening in Milton Keynes.
Council Worker	Two teenagers knifed to death.
Police Officer	Every night, chasing the same gangs. Locking up the same people. Night after night after night.
Dad	Friday, We started boxing at the local gym, Me and my son.
Council Worker	At the council, We don't believe there are gangs round here. Just groups of boys From different estates with nicknames.
Police Officer	I arrested so many damaged kids. Stuck in a world they couldn't get out of.
Dad	Saturday, A few kids joined us, boxing.
Council Worker	I put my phone away, Got back in the car.
Police Officer	I hit my limit, I saw one too many bodies on the beat.
Dad	Sunday, More kids joined. They put down the knives And picked up the gloves. Now we're boxing on every estate in Milton Keynes.

Council Worker   I breathed a sigh of relief,
                     At least it wasn't the boys I thought it was.

Police Officer   After a long shift, policing the streets,
                     I marched into my governor's office,
                     'I'm going, I'm not coming back.'

Dad   Justice isn't locking kids up,
                     It's giving them space to breathe.
                     More people should care for these kids
                     When they're alive.

Council Worker   Two teenagers, dead.
                     I carried on driving.

Dad   I mean,
                     Why do we only care about these kids
                     When they're dead?

152.

Supermarket.

Carole   Couldn't believe my eyes.
                     I was just like doing the big shop,
                     When a notification came through.

All   A man –

Lee   Sit down to eat my dinner,
                     Turn the telly on and there it was.
                     Food turned to ashes in my mouth.

All   A man, they said –

Carole   It didn't sound real.
                     Like, what the hell?

All   A man was erm –

Janet	I read about it in a newspaper,
	When I was sitting in the prison visitor
	Waiting room.
All	A man was, erm,
	Beheaded at Woodhill.

153.

Limbo.

| Ghost | Darren Williams |

Petals scatter.

154.

Supermarket.

Carole	Three prisoners,
	Armed with blades and a torn cloth.
All	Prison staff they –
Lee	All my life,
	I have fought for people
	Who can't fight for themselves.
	Why wasn't I fighting this?
All	Prison staff did nothing.
Carole	Three prisoners wrapped the cloth
	Round another guy's neck,
	Got to work cutting his head off.
All	Prison staff, too scared to intervene.
Janet	I was like,
	Sitting in the waiting room like,
	How can this actually be?

All   Prison staff just watched the whole thing.

155.

Limbo.

Ghost   I'm sorry I stopped writing,
                 I've been keeping my head down.

156.

Supermarket.

Carole   Untouchable,
                 The attackers at Woodhill
                 Said they were untouchable.

All   Shut it –

Lee   Turned the telly off.
                 It was time to fight for Kevin.

All   Shut it down –

Carole   I was shaking.
                 When that notification came through,
                 I was shell-shocked.

All   Shut it all down.

Janet   Aaron,
                 Another one of my three little birds.
                 Banged up for burglary.

                 Another one of my boys
                 Who they sent to Woodhill.

All   Shut the prison down.

157.

Limbo.

Ghost   Philip Green

Petals scatter.

158.

Otherworld.

Lights flicker.

Fellow   My work sort of involved,
Targeted research analysis around women
Who give birth in prison.

Mum   A nurse!

Advocate   I guess,
I've worked in prisons on and off
For twenty-three years.
Done some serious human rights work.

Fellow   There was this one case.
Mum was eighteen,
Gave birth alone in her cell.
She was in a private prison.

Mum   Get me a fucking nurse.

Advocate   Focusing on human standards
Makes it easier to forget
The bigger questions like,
Why are we incarcerating people anyway?

Fellow   This case was grisly, grisly, grisly.
You can probably predict
A lot of what I am going to say.

Mum	A nurse!
Advocate	Bigger questions like, Why are private companies Profiting from a system That makes people worse?
Fellow	That night, Mum pressed and pressed the cell bell. The baby wasn't breathing. No one came.
Mum	Get me a fucking nurse.
Advocate	Bigger questions like, Why are private companies Taking over state-run prisons?
Fellow	During the night, Mum had bitten through the umbilical cord While she waited for help.
Mum	A nurse!
Advocate	Bigger questions like, Does building more prisons Incentivise the powers that be To fill them up?
Fellow	In the morning An officer unlocked the cell To find Mum distraught, Holding her baby. Nurses attempted resuscitation, But it was too late. Paramedics confirmed the baby had died.
Mum	Get me a fucking nurse.
Advocate	Incarceration is not a hill Any political party wants to die on. No one will fight the battle.

Fellow	Within a year it happened again. Different mum, Different baby, Same outcome.
Mum	Get me a fucking nurse.
Advocate	So much law, So much regulation, So much oversight of our prisons. But what changes? Nothing changes. And people are still dying.
Mum	A nurse! Get me a fucking nurse.

159.

BBC Broadcasting House.

Janet	I cut back on the booze. It was time to clear my mind And face what was happening.
All	Another journalist.
Lee	Blindsided, Like a rabbit in the headlights. Where do you even begin? I started with Kevin. Told the press what it was like, Seeing the person you love fall apart.
All	Another fight.
Janet	You can't go into battle If you're lying to yourself.
All	Another interview.

Carole	Enough was enough, I was done with feeling ashamed. Chris was kept out of sight, out of mind. I had to bring my brother's story Into the light.
All	Another chance to fight for him.

160.

Limbo.

Ghost	Kevin Iverson

Petals scatter.

161.

BBC Broadcasting House.

Janet	I got a tattoo, Stephen's name on my foot.
All	Something has to give.
Lee	When Kevin died, The prison made him out to be faceless. I told the world who he really was. My deeply missed stepbrother. The man who took his life And left a hole in my heart.
All	Something is rotten.
Janet	Wherever I walk, Stephen walks with me.
All	Something must be done.

Carole	At first, It was hard to speak about Chris. Gossip gets worse the more it's spread.
	Stories were passed From one person to the next. Gossip about my brother turned into lies.
All	In those moments, He was right there with me.

162.

Limbo.

| Ghost | Don't stop fighting for me |

163.

BBC Broadcasting House.

Janet	The government sets the prison budget. Did they put a price on Stephen's head? Have they put a price on Aaron's?
All	No responsibility.
Lee	Bullheaded, I kept pushing forward with the interviews. No matter the toll on me.
All	No one was listening.
Janet	Aaron was sitting in Woodhill, Time was ticking for my boy.
All	No accountability.
Carole	Keyboard warriors Wanted their pound of flesh. The nasty comments flooded in.

Chris never hurt anyone,
But people still wanted to hurt him.

All   No,
I refuse to let sleeping dogs lie.

164.

Otherworld.

Lights flicker.

Charity Director   Sorry,
You're kind of frozen.
Can you hear me?

Here, we support bereaved families,
As they turn their grief
Into acts of resistance.

Campaigner   In this country,
A jail sentence is often a death sentence.
I campaign for change
Because we cannot go on like this.

Myatt   I can't breathe.

Charity Director   Incarceration is a system
That is not about people,
But the pursuit of profit.

Campaigner   Gareth Myatt,
A boy who loved riding his bike,
Playing chess and watching *The Simpsons*.

Myatt   I can't breathe.

Charity Director   Private companies
Are taking over prisons.
Profiting off a cruel and complacent system.

Campaigner   Gareth Myatt,
Admitted to a child prison near Northampton.
A prison run by a private security company,
Contracted by the state.

Myatt   I can't breathe.

Charity Director   Who is the most likely to be imprisoned?

Campaigner   Gareth Myatt,
A boy sentenced to custody
For breaching a community order
And stealing a bottle of beer.

Myatt   I can't breathe.

Charity Director   Who is most likely to be punished?

Campaigner   Gareth Myatt,
Refused to clean
A sandwich toaster in custody,
Officers reported he raised a fist.

Myatt   I can't breathe.

Charity Director   Who is most likely to be restrained?

Campaigner   Gareth Myatt,
Forced into a double seated restraint.
He told officers he couldn't breathe.

Charity Director   Who is the most likely to die
By the hand of the state?

Campaigner   Gareth Myatt,
Stood less than five feet tall
And weighed six and a half stone.
Officers restraining him
Weighed more than double that.

Myatt   I can't breathe

Charity Director   Imagine if we diverted money
Into people,

	Rather than putting it in the pockets of Corporate giants?
Campaigner	Gareth Myatt. Enveloped by officers with nicknames like Clubber, Crusher, Mauler and Breaker.
Myatt	I can't breathe.
Charity Director	Private companies, Profiting off a criminal justice system, That is bursting at the seams.
Campaigner	A jail sentence is often a death sentence. The state either forces your own hand, Or you are directly killed By the hand of the state.
Myatt	I can't breathe.
Charity Director	Prison is an institution Incapable of reform.
Campaigner	Gareth Myatt, Stopped breathing When he was fifteen years old.
Myatt	I can't breathe, I can't breathe, I can't breathe, I can't breathe, I can't breathe. I can't breathe, I can't breathe, I can't breathe, I can't breathe, I can't breathe.
Charity Director	Prisons? Abolish them all.

165.

Royal Courts of Justice.

Lee   It was overcast but it wasn't raining,
                That day at the Royal Courts of Justice.

All   Judges glared.

Carole   After Chris died,
                All I've ever really wanted,
                Is to stop another family
                Getting that knock at the door.

All   Judges mumbled.

Lee   Our solicitor was saying by now,
                Eighteen men had killed themselves
                At Woodhill.

All   Judges looked right through us.

Janet   In the gallery,
                I met a woman raising her granddaughter.
                Her son had died at Woodhill.
                Another mother, like me.

166.

Limbo.

Ghost   Mark Culverhouse

Petals scatter.

167.

Royal Courts of Justice.

Lee	In evidence it came out, Reports and investigations Warned the prison to change.
All	Woodhill failed to keep men safe.
Carole	Angry, I was just so fucking angry. I never want anyone to feel this pain.
All	Woodhill failed to stop the deaths.
Lee	In evidence it came out, Death investigations raised the same issues, Over and over again.
All	Woodhill failed to learn from its mistakes.
Janet	Sitting shoulder to shoulder With so many families, I didn't feel so alone anymore.

168.

Limbo.

Ghost   Andriejus Kostiajevas

Petals scatter.

169.

Royal Courts of Justice.

| Lee | The Ministry of Justice
Blamed it all on the prison staff.
Chucked them all under the bus. |
| All | Systems tossed our boys in jail. |

Carole	Judges said human error killed our boys. Like, it was down to prison officers failing To operate within the system. Do you know what I mean?
All	Systems ignored the warning signs.
Lee	In court, I could feel justice for Kevin slipping away.
Janet	I looked at the judges In their wigs and gowns. And I just wanted to scream for our boys.
	Who hasn't made a mistake? Who hasn't done Something wrong in their life?
	If you find me that person, I will show you a liar.
All	Systems left our boys to die.
Janet	For the grace of God, This could be your life. This could be your dance.
All	It could be you.

170.

Limbo.

Ghost	Bulent Sessacar

Petals scatter.

171.

Otherworld.

Lights flicker.

Solicitor Coffee?
       I'm sorry, do you take sugar?

Legal Adviser Law and justice are not the same.
       I say that quite a lot to the prisoners
       Who call our advice line.

Barrister As barristers,
       We sign up to the cab rank rule.
       If you're available and capable
       To take the case,
       You say yes.

Solicitor Every single family
       I have represented in court,
       One of the first things they say to me is,
       We want other families
       To be spared this pain.

Legal Adviser Phone rings.

Barrister Cages,
       My clients are kept in cages within cages.
       Fed through a hatch.

Solicitor Woodhill is not a one-off.
       It's happening everywhere.
       I meet bereaved families
       From all over the country.

Legal Adviser Another case.

Barrister Stripped,
       My client's personality and humanity
       Is stripped away.
       Until they feel nothing inside.

Solicitor Every time bereaved families
       Hear of another death,
       It makes them feel their loved one
       Died in vain.

Legal Adviser	Phone rings.
Barrister	Breeding, What are we breeding in these cages within cages?
Solicitor	The High Court ruling Could have changed everything. But the court ruled against the families. Deaths at Woodhill did stop For a little while though. But then they carried on again.
Legal Adviser	Phone rings.
Barrister	I guess the problem is, No one cares What being in a cage does to someone. Until the cages are opened And the men are released again.
Solicitor	Truth is, We're all just patching holes, Not saving lives.
Legal Adviser	Phone rings, another case.
Barrister	Aren't prisons supposed to keep us all safe?
Solicitor	Thirty-three suicides at Woodhill. Thirty-three bereaved families. Thirty-three souls.
Legal Adviser	Phone rings, another case.

172.

Limbo.

Janet	Earth

| Lee | To |
| Carole | Earth |

173.

Graveyard.

| Carole | At the undertakers, |
| | Chris just looked wrong. |

Mum and me asked the funeral director,
To cremate my brother with his hood up.

And that was him,
That's how Chris will forever be.

Head down, hood up.

174.

Limbo.

Janet	Ashes
Lee	To
Carole	Ashes

175.

Graveyard.

| Lee | I come from a butcher's family. |
| | We view death differently. |

It comes to us all.
Death is gonna come one day.

Kevin is earth now and that's it.

176.

Limbo.

Janet	Dust
Lee	To
Carole	Dust

177.

Graveyard.

Janet	Lads on Stephen's wing Did a collection for some funeral flowers. Boys from the rugby club carried the coffin. Aaron couldn't do it, Cos he was in cuffs.
	Nathan and Sophia held my hand. I didn't want them to let go.
	The service ended. That was when it hit me, My son was never coming back.
All	He was never coming home.

178.

Limbo.

Janet	In sure
Lee	And certain hope
Carole	Of the Resurrection to eternal life.

179.

Graveyard.

Lee   I can't let go.

180.

Otherworld.

Lights flicker.

Partner   Lee?

181.

Graveyard.

Lee   I can't let go,
                 Till I get justice for Kevin.

182.

Otherworld.

Lights flicker.

Partner   Lee?

183.

Graveyard.

Lee   Lynsey?

184.

Otherworld.

Lights flicker.

Partner   Lee?
                 Nothing changes.

185.

Graveyard.

Lee   Another interview.

186.

Otherworld.

Lights flicker.

Partner   Every time there's another death at
                 Woodhill,
                 The house gets busy.

                 Lee does another interview
                 In the sitting room
                 But nothing changes.

187.

Graveyard.

Lee   I tell the story.

188.

Otherworld.

Lights flicker.

Partner   Story.
                   I hate the word 'story'.

189.

Graveyard.

Lee   Another interview.

190.

Otherworld.

Lights flicker.

Partner   This isn't a story,
                   It's real life.

191.

Graveyard.

Lee   I tell the story.

192.

Otherworld.

Lights flicker.

Partner   Like,
                   Does anyone really listen?

193.

Graveyard.

Lee   Another interview.

194.

Otherworld.

Lights flicker.

Partner   Do people actually care?

195.

Graveyard.

Lee   I tell the story.

196.

Otherworld.

Lights flicker.

Partner   Or is this just another story?

197.

Graveyard.

Lee   Another interview.

198.

Otherworld.

Lights flicker.

Partner	Nothing changes.
	The past cannot be undone,
	It's time for us to move on.

199.

Graveyard.

Lee	I tell the story.

200.

Otherworld.

Lights flicker.

Partner	But we can't.
	So, we are trapped.
	Trapped in the story.

201.

Graveyard.

Lee	I tell and tell and tell the story.

202.

Otherworld.

Lights flicker.

Partner   Good luck with your play.

203.

Graveyard.

Janet   Say his name
Lee   I can't let go
Carole   Keep him alive

204.

Limbo.

Ghost   I love you

205.

Graveyard.

Janet   Say his name
Lee   I can't let go,
Carole   Keep him alive

206.

Limbo.

Ghost   I miss you

207.

Graveyard.

Janet	Say his name
Lee	I can't let go
Carole	Keep him alive

208.

Limbo.

Ghost	I'll see you on the other side

209.

Graveyard.

Janet	Say
Lee	His
Carole	Name

210.

Limbo.

Janet	Stephen Phillip Owen Farrar
All	Let them go
Carole	Christopher John Carpenter
All	Let them go
Lee	Kevin Christopher Scarlett

All   Let them go

Flowers scatter.

211.

Otherworld.

Lights flicker.

Dictaphone clicks.

Janet   So,
               Are we recording now?

Lee   Yeah, they're gonna hear our real voices.

Carole   What?
               Our proper words?

Janet   Well,
               I've spent so many years,
               Trying to get to the bottom
               Of who killed my son.

Lee   Who killed my stepbrother?

Carole   Who killed my brother?

Janet   The dust has settled.

Lee   And now I see.

Carole   It wasn't just the prison.

Janet   Or the politicians.

Lee   Or even the state.

Carole   It was kind of all of us,
               Do you know what I mean?

Janet   Yeah, in our erm complacency

Lee	In our ignorance.
Carole	In our silence.
Janet	So now, I offer you my story.
Lee	I give you my words.
Carole	I refuse to be voiceless anymore.
Janet	Take my hand.
Lee	And I will take yours.
Carole	Don't leave me on this lonely road.
Janet	Fight for Stephen.
Lee	Keep Kevin in your heart.
Carole	Don't forget Chris's name.
Janet	I couldn't live with myself If our boys died for nothing.
Lee	There has to be a reason.
Carole	Something has to come from all this hurt.
Janet	Okay, shall we stop now?
Lee	Yeah, we have to.
Carole	Sure, okay.
Janet	Let's end this. Cos I'm about to scream This whole fucking building down.

Ghost turns out the lights.

Afterword

England and Wales's imprisonment rates are the second highest in Western Europe, beaten only by Scotland. After former Justice Secretary Chris Grayling's 2012 benchmarking policy generated historic staff reductions, England and Wales's prisons became less safe than ever recorded. 2016 saw record suicide numbers, which were followed by record levels of prisoner self-harm year on year.

Amidst this sorry picture, HMP Woodhill combined: a local prison function, a high-security unit and a close supervision centre for 'disruptive' prisoners. It combined these three complex functions at the sharpest end of staff cuts, with staff retention and recruitment efforts in declining conditions being particularly compromised by the number of alternative jobs in Milton Keynes and easily accessible London.

England and Wales's towering imprisonment rates significantly over-represent people with serious mental illness and disabilities, even when their criminal responsibility is deeply questionable.

Mr Jason Basalat died at HMP Woodhill on 11th December 2016 at fifty-two years old. He was arrested two days before, having grabbed a coach steering wheel after panicking because he believed people with guns and bombs on the coach were trying to kill him. He told the police that he had paranoid schizophrenia yet was remanded to Northamptonshire Magistrates Court, from where he was remanded to Woodhill 'for his own protection'.

Jason Basalat survived in prison for less than twenty-four hours. Sadly, Jason Basalat's death is far from the only example of people with very severe mental illness who went on to take their own lives whilst imprisoned on remand.

Reading these cases, hearing families' words, knowing this happens, needlessly, again and again and again, is simply devastating. Even in the most well-resourced prison systems, the stress of being imprisoned can induce psychological disturbance, even amongst those with no prior disorder.

The UK is the sixth richest national economy in the world. The British education system is reputed to have one of the highest education standards in the world. We can do better than this. But instead, we are planning to wildly increase the prison population, perhaps by more than 25 per cent before the decade is out. How many more families will have to go through this?

Professor Philippa Tomczak
Director of the prison HEALTH group
at the University of Nottingham.

Get Support

If you, or someone you know, have been affected by bereavement or are experiencing suicidal thoughts, the following organisations may be able to help.

Cruse Bereavement Care

Cruse Bereavement Care provides support after the death of someone close including face to face, telephone, group support, as well as bereavement support for children.

Phone: 0808 808 1677 (England, Wales and Northern Ireland) or 0808 802 6161 (Scotland)

Website: www.cruse.org.uk

Survivors of Bereavement by Suicide

Survivors of Bereavement by Suicide exists to meet the needs and break the isolation of those bereaved by the suicide of a close relative or friend.

Phone: 0115 944 1117

Website: www.uksobs.org

Samaritans

Samaritans works to make sure there's always someone there for anyone who needs someone. Whatever you're going through, call them for free anytime.

Phone: 116 123

Website: www.samaritans.org

National Suicide Prevention Alliance

The NSPA is an alliance of over 1,700 individuals and public, private, voluntary and community organisations in England who care about suicide prevention and are willing to take action to reduce suicide and those affected by suicide.

Website: www.nspa.org.uk

Specialist Advice and Support

If your loved one has died in police or prison custody, immigration detention or in mental health settings, support is available. You can also find out more about how to campaign alongside families and others to access the truth, hold those responsible to account and effect meaningful change to prevent future deaths.

INQUEST

INQUEST is the only charity providing expertise on state related deaths and their investigation to bereaved people, lawyers, advice and support agencies, the media and parliamentarians.

Phone: 020 7263 1111 (option 1 for new enquiries, option 2 if you have a caseworker)

Website: www.inquest.org.uk